LETTER FROM THE EDITORS

    This Hispanic History Month, step into the stories and art work of the YOUNG IGNORANTES Latinx community. We are different and diverse and have all lived lives completely seperate from the experiences of each other. We all have vastly different stories to tell and hold fast to this diversity that makes our people so unique and so beautiful.

    In a time where some of us live in a country that will break our backs to build a future they don't want us in, it's important for us to control our own narrative and to scream it from every rooftop. And in a time where some of us have to flee our homes for a better life, it's important to remember who we are and to fight for each other when no one else will.

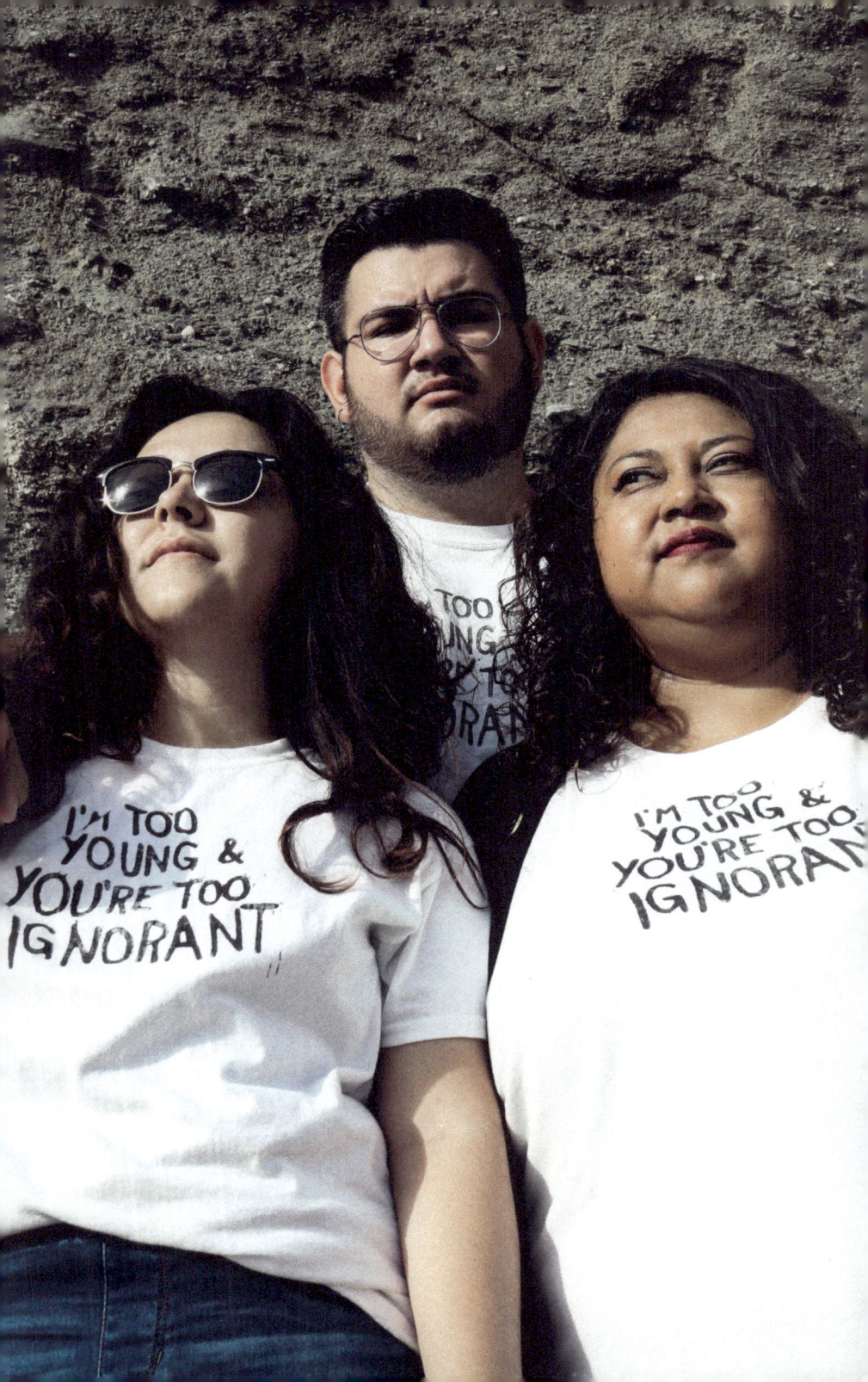

5	MELISSA ARELLANO
9	THE VICE COLUMN
10	ELLAS
11	MY BROWN SKIN
12	MATT BRADY
17	INTERNACIONAL
18	WHO AM I?
19	RETURN TO ME
21	CLAUDIA RAMOS
25	ANCHOR BABY
29	VICTORIA MOLINA VARGAS

EDITORIAL SHOOT
Photographer: Josephine Jael Jimenez
Models: Melissa Arellano, Matt Brady, Claudia Ramos

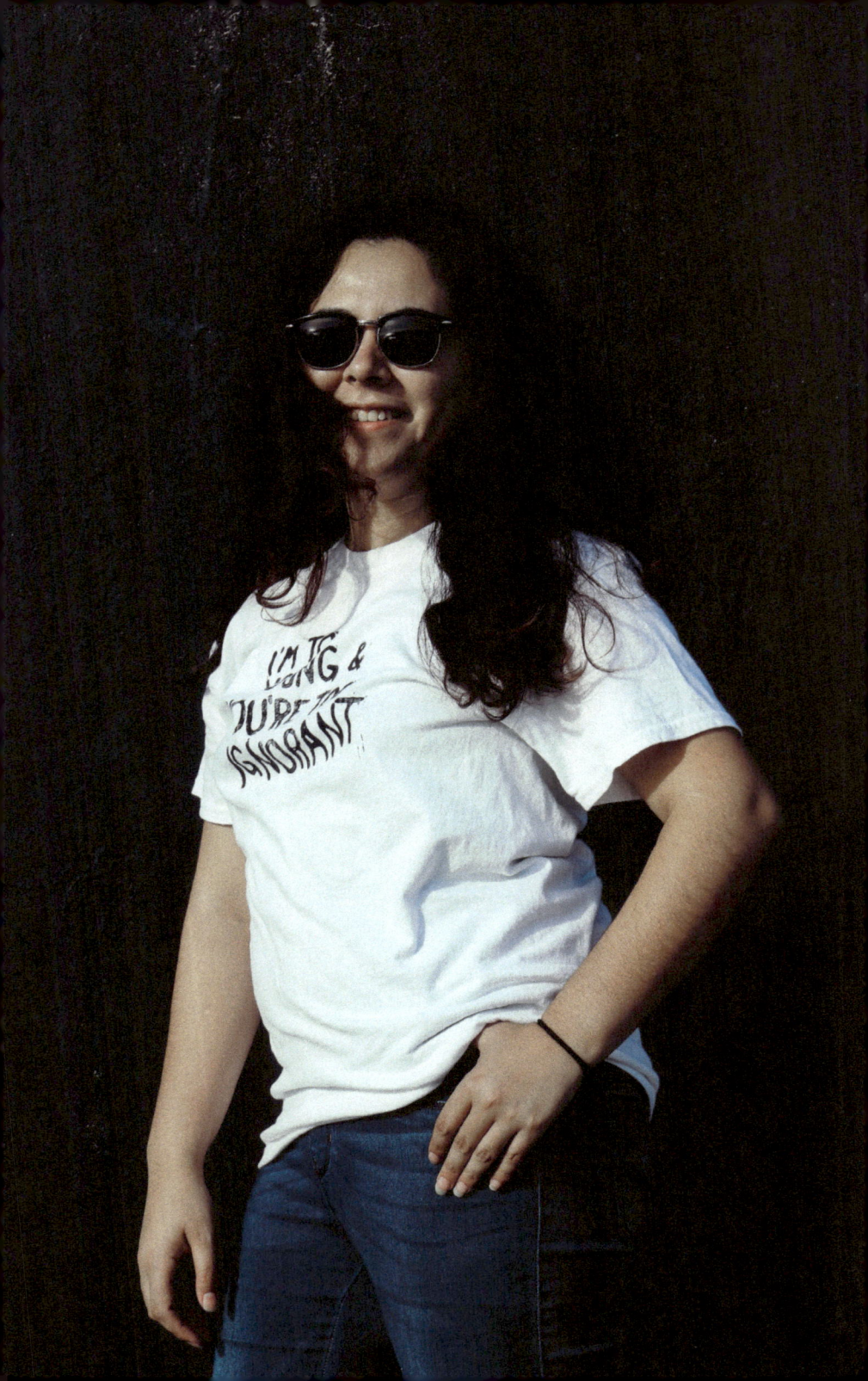

Melissa Arellano's Poetry is the Voice to Your Dark Feelings

BRENDA HERNÁNDEZ JAIMES

Are you haunted by the ghosts of lost loves? Have you ever suffered the asphyxiation of wearing the heavy mask that conceals your sorrow? Or emotionally bleeding from the torture caused by your inner demons? You'll discover solace and a voice to all the raging emotions in your soul with Melissa Arellano's poetry. As an introspective young Latina, Melissa's voice is clear and powerful while baring her heart and emotions in her poems.

"When I write my poems, I write how I'm feeling, and a lot of times things you don't normally say. Like you wouldn't go around telling someone that you feel suicidal, you don't go around telling someone that you're depressed. Maybe after a breakup, months have passed and everybody thinks that you're okay and moved on. You're not going around telling people that you're still sad because most of the times either people don't care or don't give you the answers that you're looking for. That's why I put so much emotion in my poems," Melissa shares.

It was in middle school when she came across poetry from listening to Eminem's rap. The way he would make his words rhyme to tell a story piqued Melissa's curiosity of what he would rhyme next. During her English class, her teacher opened up a poetry submission which motivated Melissa to send her poems in hopes of being recognized by her like-minded teacher.

"When I turned them in, the teacher accused me of plagiarism in front of the whole class," she says and goes on to share that she defended her work, "I put all my heart into this project because I loved it and enjoyed it. Overall it was such a great effort and it was fantastic. It just made me feel I got the short end of the stick," she says, "I didn't get any feedback. So, that kind of killed my dreams a little bit. I think she was racist because there was this other girl who had blonde hair, blue eyes, and freckles. When she submitted her portfolio, she praised her in front of the whole class, but going from there I used that anger to keep writing more poems."

Poetry became her catharsis and even though she felt shot down, the accusation motivated her to continue writing. "She accused me of plagiarism, that must mean my poems are that good if she thought they had been published poems," Melissa continues, "I kind of looked at it that

> "...love yourself and be proud of yourself and keep going no matter what, keep going."

way instead of the more negative way. That did kind of pushed me a little bit and the fact that she was racist so that kind of angered me and fueled me in to keep going and keep writing. You know even if no one reads it that's good enough for me."

Melissa posted her poems on Facebook, Power Poetry and Instagram, but rarely received any feedback, which deflated her enthusiasm. It wasn't until her last relationship that her ex-boyfriend took an interest in her poems and connected with the pieces that covered depression and suicide.

"That made me feel like, if he loves me and he loves what I'm expressing in my poems then maybe they're that good to be heard," she says and goes on to share that it was that relationship that had caused her to feel lost and ultimately made her stop writing for many years. Fortunately, she continues to write her poems and is a collaborator for Young Ignorantes.

"I wanted to kind of write my story, sort of like, to warn or to help girls in my shoes. I started writing letters to my ex, 'You know I understand that you couldn't deal with it. We were going through hard times.' I put all my regrets and sadness into all those letters and from the letters, I went back to the poems," she confesses. "I mean a letter is a good way to explain everything and tell a story. I could explain to my ex, 'Yeah, you made me feel like this and this.' A poem is short and sweet and gets to the point. I felt I could express more with the little words and the little phrases rather than writing huge letters."

"After the letters, I started writing poems. Then again, I didn't post them and kept them to myself. I felt like, 'No one is going to read this. They're going to think I'm crazy," Melissa says laughing, "I never shared those poems and eventually my ex came back and he left again. That happened a couple of years ago. Then I didn't share those poems until Joey."

Latinx writer, producer, and Young Ignorantes collaborator, Joey Reyes, posted that we were accepting submissions and Melissa saw it as an opportunity to share her work and receive the feedback she had been yearning for.

"I was like, 'oh let me try it! Maybe they'll like it, maybe they won't but maybe I'll find out if I'm good enough or not!' And I submitted to the first one, but I think I missed the deadline," she laughs. "I cut it very close. And I was like, 'Oh, maybe it's because I missed the deadline. And from that submission that I sent, you used it for the next issue. And I was like, 'Oh shit!' and I kept submitting them and I was like, 'Okay, they must like them, I guess!' I don't know, I'm probably doing something right. It gave me that boost, like, 'okay, maybe my poems are worthy of being heard!'"

Melissa is currently a steady collaborator for Young Ignorantes, one of the cover models for our LATINIDAD issue and studying in the Diagnostic Medical Sonography Program. She's planning to work as a technician in a women's clinic or a general hospital. As for her creative work, Melissa envisions to have her poetry book published.

"Kind of what I want to do with my poems is something good to come out from being sad or angry. So rather than be depressed and waste a couple of hours and hate myself afterward I was like, 'Well I'm depressed like shit, let me write some shitty ass poems. You know hopefully one day someone will read it.' And I like that, the fact that someone can read it and say, 'you know what, yeah I feel what you feel and I understand.' My cousin too, because I showed her that I wrote for the other issues of Young Ignorantes and she was like, 'That touched my soul' especially because she was going through a breakup and said, 'yeah, I really feel what you felt,'" she says and encourages our fellow Latinas that might be in a dark place to find the strength within themselves and not rely on other people's opinions.

"Keep trying no matter what you do. Even if it's just writing one line every night or having a journal and writing, 'I'm depressed or I'm sad.' It' doesn't matter, keep writing! How sad? What's making you sad? What can you do to make yourself feel better? Nothing, okay well what's causing you more sadness? Drinking. Okay, find a way to stop drinking, to stop smoking or stop running from your feelings. It's okay to be sad, it's okay to be angry. You can't go out and punch the guy in the face, but you can punch his face in a poem or a story," Melissa advises. "Do something constructive when you're feeling down because later when you look back at it you won't think it was time wasted. You acknowledge I was going through a process and this was able to come from that process and I built on top of that or maybe you'll find something else. Maybe you're writing poems and it's just not working out, maybe you'll get published in a zine and meet an artist and all of a sudden discover you like painting. You know there are different branches to different paths to take. Just don't give up on yourself and keep going. That above all love yourself because someone that loves you may leave tomorrow, but you're always with you. Just love yourself and be proud of yourself and keep going no matter what, keep going."

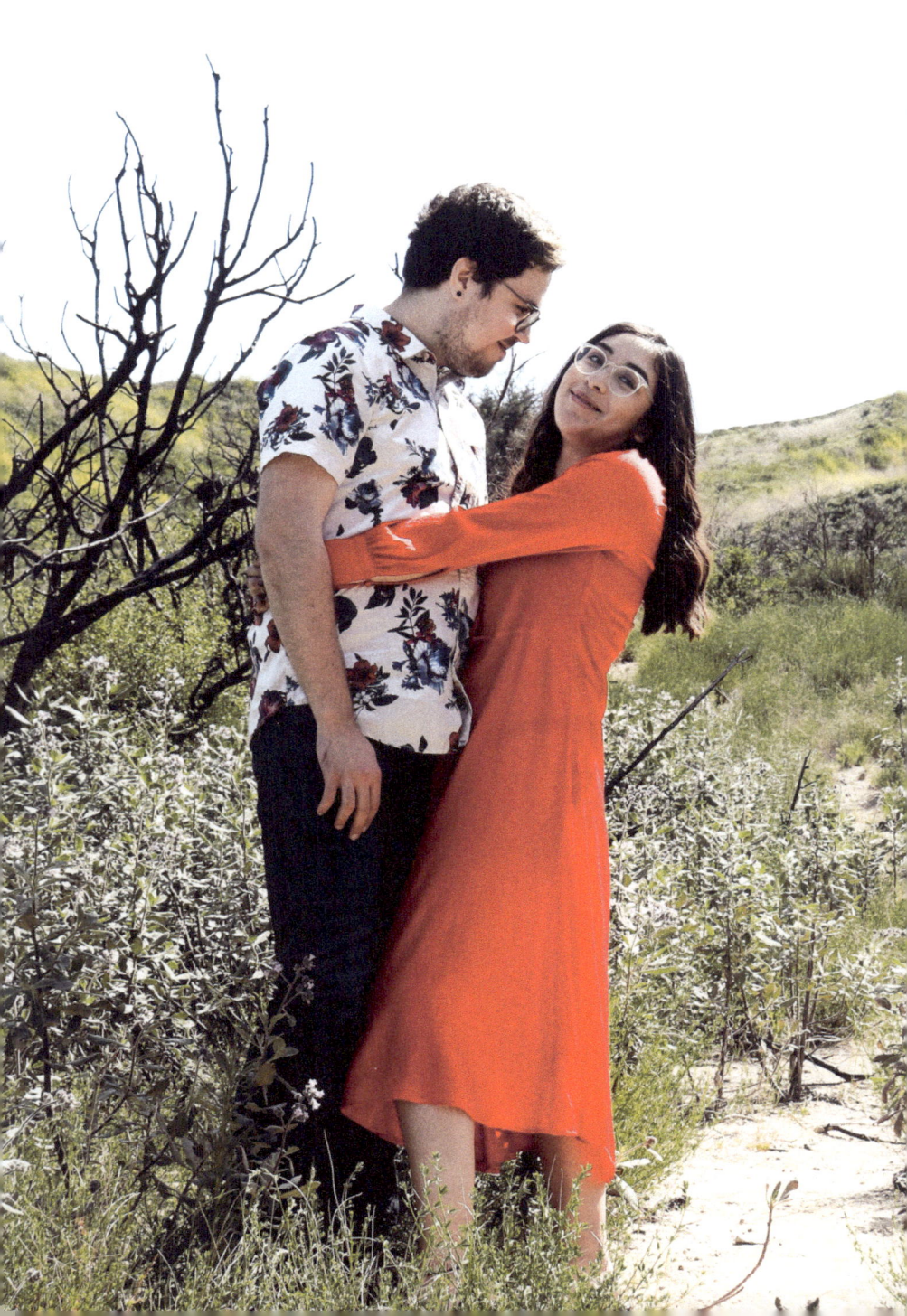

THE VICE COLUMN

Making fun of white people.

Josephine Jael Jimenez

You know what I love? Making fun of white people. It's an addiction, really. I don't know how to stop making fun of the shit they say and the shit they do. It wasn't a huge issue, really. My friends had gotten used to it and would tell me to stop when necessary. Some even started laughing along. But now I love and live with a white guy and it's not going over so well.

It started off innocent enough and I definitely stand by the things I say because I know my perspective as a First Gen Mexican-American woman matters, but people say I don't always have to make it about race. He says his feelings get hurt because I'm making fun of the way he grew up, his heritage.

To some extent, I know I could dial it back a bit. I could stop saying his people's food is terrible and that his people colonized and raped and killed mine, but sometimes I feel stubborn enough to just not feel like it.

But it's not just that we grew up differently or that he was given a better slice of life than me through generational wealth and through being a tall, cis-white man. Sometimes we argue about the mannerisms he inherited from a society that was built around him.

"You shouldn't wait for people to get out of your way when you're walking down the street. You should side step them."

"You shouldn't step in people's paths expecting them to let you pass. Slow down and look where you're walking."

It's the little things that I notice because I'm a woman. Men always expect us to make way for them in the street. Try it sometime. They'll run into you before they even think to make way for you both to pass safely. It's a societal game of chicken we've been letting men passively win for years. Most men I know don't even recognize it until they start paying attention. I suppose I expected my partner to be better than that.

But deep down, I feel tiny ripples of pleasure when I call him out on his white bullshit, his male mannerisms. It feels like I get to force him and mold him into this lovely little woke piece of jewelry I get to wear on my neck.

"Hey, look at me, I fixed a white guy."

I shouldn't hurt my partner's feelings to get him to wake up to the reality of being a woman of color. He's never been and will never be a woman of color. He's not going to learn the experiences that have molded me throughout my life in one single argument. It's going to take time, just like it took time for me to learn how to live in a world that was catered to and made for people like him.

This addiction of mine, to call out white people for the sins of their ancestors can be productive, but it can also be destructive in the context of an interracial relationship. My vice may not be lethal, but it could be. All I need to do is be more gentle, but my culture never taught me that.

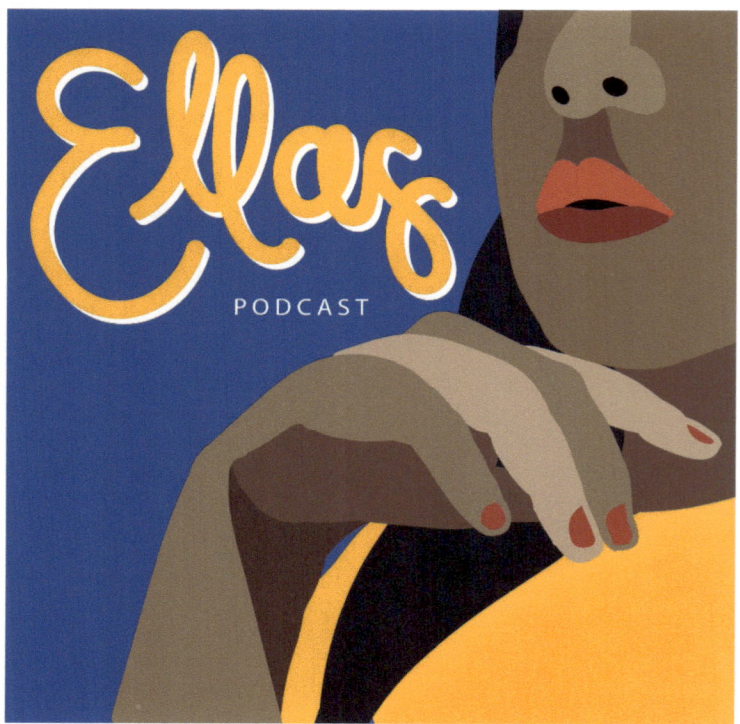

    Ellas is a bi-weekly podcast hosted by Brenda Hernández Jaimes. As a podcast made by Latinas for Latinas, Brenda talks with talented, inspiring, and empowering women that are living their dreams and making a path for the next generation.

    The mission with Ellas is to provide a platform to these women to share their stories of facing obstacles, overcoming them and the goals that they've accomplished. On each episode, Brenda converses with women who have encountered many challenges in their path. From language barriers to schooling, discrimination, personal and professional roadblocks.

    Ellas is focused on bringing forth the strong voices of these women and have their stories encourage our current and future generation of Latinas to continue their pursuit with their professional and personal goals. And most importantly to remind us that we are not alone.

MY BROWN SKIN
JOEY REYES

My brown skin
Is beautiful
Too precious to live in fear
Too powerful to be kept in cages
Too rooted in this land to be told to go anywhere else

My brown skin
Is indigenous
Mexica Gods and Goddesses
Bless me each and every day
My legacy is their legacy
An existence that, despite ignorance and hatred,
continues to seep it's roots deep into the rich ground

My brown mind
Is formed
Through comida, familia, música
Pieces of Indigenous, African, and European customs
mixed together to form a limitless and expansive gente

Our black & brown stories
Are boldly told
By Frida Kahlo, and Celia Cruz, Yalitza Aparicio, and José Rivera, and Sandra
Cisneros, and Luis Alfaro, and Guadalís del Carmen, and Issac Gómez, and
Georgina Escobar, and Nelson Díaz Marcano, and Andrew Rincón, and Charise
Castro Smith, and and and…

My brown soul
Expands into the universe
Every time I taste my Nana's arroz con leche
Every time I see my black and brown family
Every time I hear a rolled R followed by a lip lined smile
Every time I feel the vibrations of mariachis fuel my hips
Every time I smell fresh conchas at the panadería
Every time my brown mother interlocks eyes with me and says,
"I love you. I'm proud of you."

My brown legacy is
Cortez
Martínez
Reyes
Torres

My brown skin is beautiful
My brown skin is home
My brown skin is magic
My brown skin is
Forever

12

Lessons in Plant Science and Agriculture Labor with Matt Brady

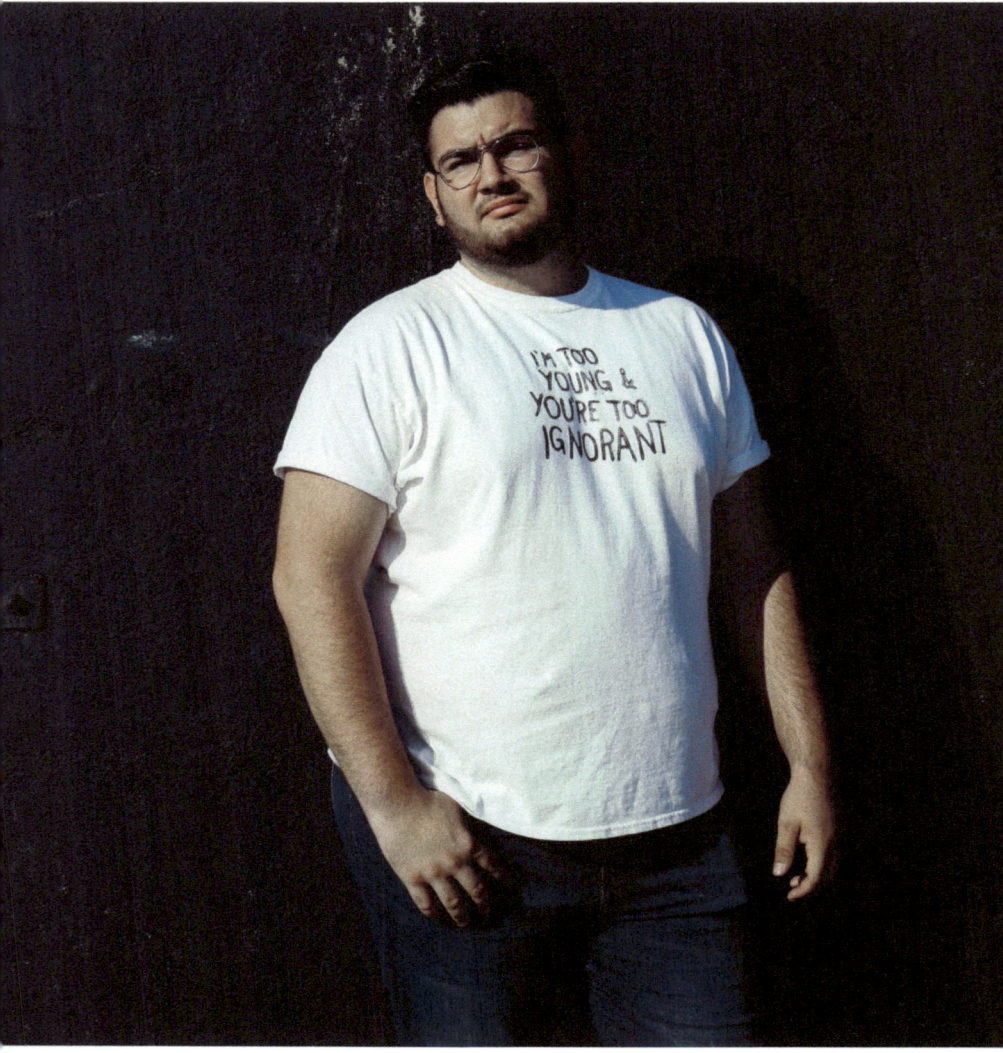

BRENDA HERNÁNDEZ JAIMES

When it comes to green spaces, agriculture's intricate labor aspect towards migrant workers, and the unbalanced force of impact between social classes, is a conversation that is spoken in our Latino community, but muted in white spaces. Matt Brady, a Plant Science student of Mexican descent from Cal State Poly Pomona is passionate about these crucial topics and how people should inform themselves to see the bigger picture to properly communicate and help the communities affected During his summer internship in Alaska, these issues crossed his mind while cleaning flower buds with water and baking soda for 10 hours a day, 7 days a week - without any breaks in a 30° flower cooler. His work was not only physically draining, but also mentally and emotionally challenging for him.

"These migrant workers and immigrants don't have the same privileges as we do to take time for themselves. For them, time is money and if they can't get 60 boxes of strawberry, they aren't going to get a decent paycheck," Matt informs, "They're all paid per pound or volume, and not hourly. They don't have the same luxury as we do. A lot of the times they don't have the same rights either - they don't have overtime pay. Agriculture workers are the least paid workers in all the United States, and they're also the least compensated in what they do."

Matt goes on to explain that there's also a pro and con in companies maintaining a cheap labor cost, it helps keep food prices down for everyone, specifically for people living in the city that depend on WIC and EBT. Without it, the low-income bracket either gets to eat or they don't while middle and upper class see it more as a nuisance.

"The government also realizes that, so it doesn't have as many implementations and regulations for agricultural workers as they do for everyone else. I mean I understand both sides because, on one hand, you want to be able to give a living wage and have them provide for their families without killing themselves," he says. "It's kind of a messed up thing because someone loses on either side and its people from the same low-income social bracket, but it's one side or the other. Which side are you going to shit on basically."

"For someone like me, I can bring awareness and people have, but it's not going to change the whole system," Matt informs disappointedly. "The system is fundamentally broken in many different ways and I don't think people realize how broken it is. Even activists - I understand them trying to bring awareness to issues they're passionate about, but it's just not that issue. It's a whole spiderweb of issues that are interconnected with each other, and focusing on one of them isn't necessarily going to fix the problem, it's just putting a band-aid on it. For me, it's just a hard way to tackle it, even while looking at sustainability in agriculture."

In his own words, Matt Brady is a guy from Downey, California, who is "nothing too special". However, the way he's able to articulate these issues with his vast knowledge says otherwise. As the youngest sibling of two, he grew up as an only child and was looked after by his parents and older sister, who is 18 years older than him and like a second mother. While she had grown up with their maternal grandmother, who had taught her Spanish, his grandmother passed away before she could teach him. Growing up as a biracial, second-generation Latino who is part of the LGBTQ+ community in a predominantly Hispanic high school, he was rejected by his peers for not "looking Mexican" and not speaking Spanish.

"My grandparents immigrated from Mexico and they're like, 'but you don't look like it', and that doesn't matter. It's still part of my culture. Unfortunately, within my family, it got lost a little bit, but I'm still part of it. Yes some people can't speak Spanish and it sucks but that isn't necessarily a reflection of who that person is. If that person comes from that culture, accepts that culture, and makes it their own, then let them embrace it," Matt says passionately. "They're not appropriating that culture because that is their culture. It's their birthright, you can't tell them no because they grew up in a different situation then they did. It's still their bloodline, they're still a part of it and don't deny someone for having a different experience. People come from different experiences and people are genuinely individualistic. No one is going to be the same as you. Don't demonize a person because they want to accept their culture but they don't speak the same as you or look the same as you."

Matt is currently studying his fifth year in Cal State Poly Pomona, one of the best agriculture schools in the state and has beaten Penn State in turf competitions. As for his future, Matt faces his challenges. By the time he graduates in May 2020, he'll have student debt to repay and looking for a job in the plant science sector that will make him money.

"I'm very passionate about focusing on food desserts, doing urban agriculture, and being able to have people who don't have access to fresh food and vegetables gain access to that, but it doesn't make you money. I have a debt that I need to repay, so I have to focus on that before I can do anything else," Matt says. "For me, it's just repaying that debt before anything. It kind of sucks, because I didn't receive any financial aid. I received a couple of scholarships, but it was based on where I was at the time. My parents make too much for the system, but they don't make enough to help through college. So I'm stuck in this place of well I need a degree, kind of, because in our generation if you don't have a degree, you're not getting any work. But I have no help in obtaining that so I have to put myself in debt so I can obtain that, and pay that off and be able to do what I want to do. For me, it sucks, because I would love to go out and be a community worker and work in these places, but it's just not realistic. For me, goal wise it's just getting a job to be able to pay off my debt and be able to, maybe, sometime in the future help the people that I want to help now."

For anyone interested in studying plant science, he highly recommends exploring and getting involved in the workplace by interning for their local farmers' markets, community events, and nonprofits to discover their passion before stepping in a four-year university program. He also advises to research and knows exactly what area of plant science to study. It can range from irrigation which focuses on turf and is golf course management, agronomy entails growing food crops, horticulture is all ornamental plants in greenhouses and ornamental nurseries, floriculture is essentially growing flowers or even focus on the business side of plants, but centered on the marketing aspect. He also talks about how the academic and business sides of agriculture are white-owned, but it's a vital and perfect moment to show your abilities, knowledge, and worth to these people.

"We don't realize it because we're in Southern California and we have a very diverse background, but I've gone to a bunch of conferences like The National Collegiate Landscape Competition. It was held in Colorado last year and I didn't realize how diverse SoCal is compared to everywhere until I went there. Our team was mostly Latinx people and we had the most women on our team as well. It was definitely an eye-opener, but just know that your gender and skin color shouldn't make a difference in what you want to accomplish," Matt encourages. "If you put your mind to it and make those connections with people then you can overcome those boundaries that other people put up for you. It's going to be difficult and it's going to be hard, but it will be a lot harder than some people in privilege. It will be worth it in the end because you will pave the way for other people and be an example to them and show them to go after their dreams as well."

Matt also recognizes he doesn't necessarily face the same challenges as other people. He comes from a place of privilege and is a cis white man that is straight presenting.

"I also embrace my diversity with being a Latinx within the LGBT+ community being part of that and bringing those issues to the table," he says. "Using that privilege to shed light on that and being able to open a conversation about these issues. It sucks that discrimination is a thing, it sucks that there are limitations based on socio-economic class based on skin color. I just want everybody to able to do and become the people they want to be no matter what. That's what I'm working towards, letting people be themselves, and being who they want to be."

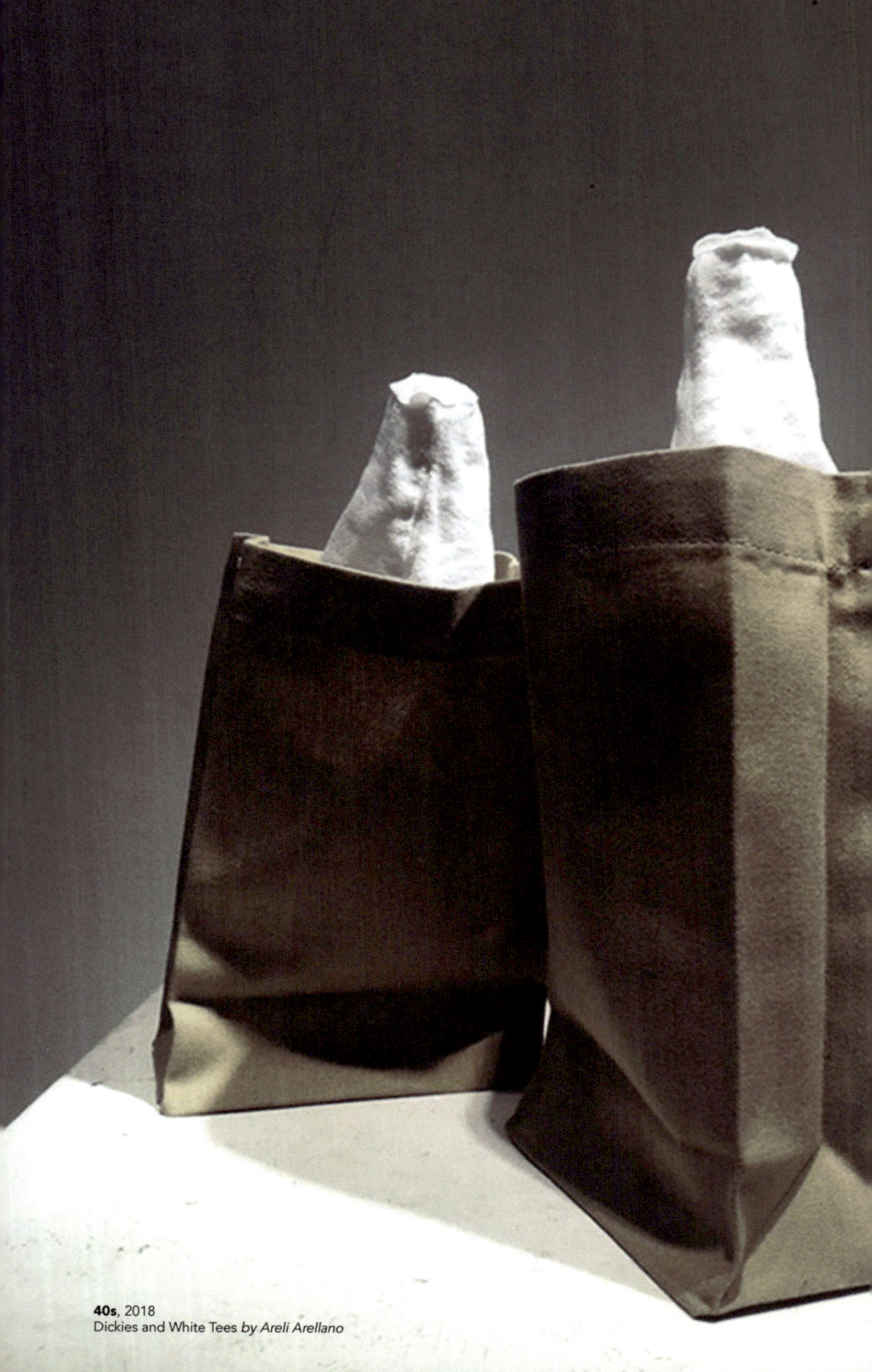

40s, 2018
Dickies and White Tees by Areli Arellano

Internacional
ALEJANDRA CÁRCAMO

Las costas del sur envolverán mis pies.
Déjenme nutrir con mi sudor la tierra
al llenarse de vida un tamboril.

Otras palabras danzan en mi lengua
se mueven,
inmigrantes
primitivas
tan naturales.

Sin pensar, me dejo abducir por la luz
de una ciudad siempre hiperactiva,
tomo historias de distintos rincones
y las clavo en la mirada de un extraño.

Las calles, los aviones y autobuses
se convierten en una extensión de mí.
El alma se me va otra vez de viaje y yo,
pierdo, encuentro y vuelvo a transitar.

WHO AM I?

Melissa Arellano

Who am I?
I am a Latina.
I am a girl with a lion's mane
and a corazón that refuses to be tamed.
Mi sangre es de fuego,
it ignites los sueños de mi imaginación,
y se enciende y fortalece mi corazón.
Un corazón lleno de sueños, amor y esperanza.
Soy la hija de padres que nunca se rindieron
Y por eso soy orgullosa
Por eso soy quien soy.
I am a girl with a lion's mane
And a bleeding heart
That refuses to be tame.

Return to me

SARAH RIZVI

I want to call you
to delete every picture I sent
You no longer deserve those private smiles
The unique curve of the chin
As it connects to the crooked dimples
The result of my lost retainer
Those don't belong to you
                      are not for you anymore
Fuck but then I want you to show up on my doorstep
At the Starbucks across from my work
With a ring, sunflowers, and the dried mangoes I like

I want to call you
tell you to shred the letter you're in the middle of writing
                                    You know, to save me the trouble
Say with a straight face that I don't need your handwritten note for closure
                All the while I see flashes of your journal every time I close my eyes
The page where you finally said you were ready to marry me stands out as the least pixelated

I want to call you
to cradle my face between your hands
"This is not your fault"
"I'm sorry I lied about being a family"
"I wasn't man enough to keep you and you deserve better"
"Know that there will never be another chance like the one your love gave me"
"You were the love of my life and I will always regret the day I let you go"
I hear a phantom voice whisper in your accent
That fucking voice
So resolute yet invisible
Like the hands that touched me for the last time in the LAX parking lot
Like the tears shed on my couch

I want to call you
But I would need a medium for that
You left my world long ago
And this pain
This grief
           is the anesthesia wearing off
Our constructed life a drug-induced sleep
When I wake up
When I wake
You will have surgically planted my heart back
The doctors will help with the transition
But for the surgery to be a success there can be
no foreign bodies

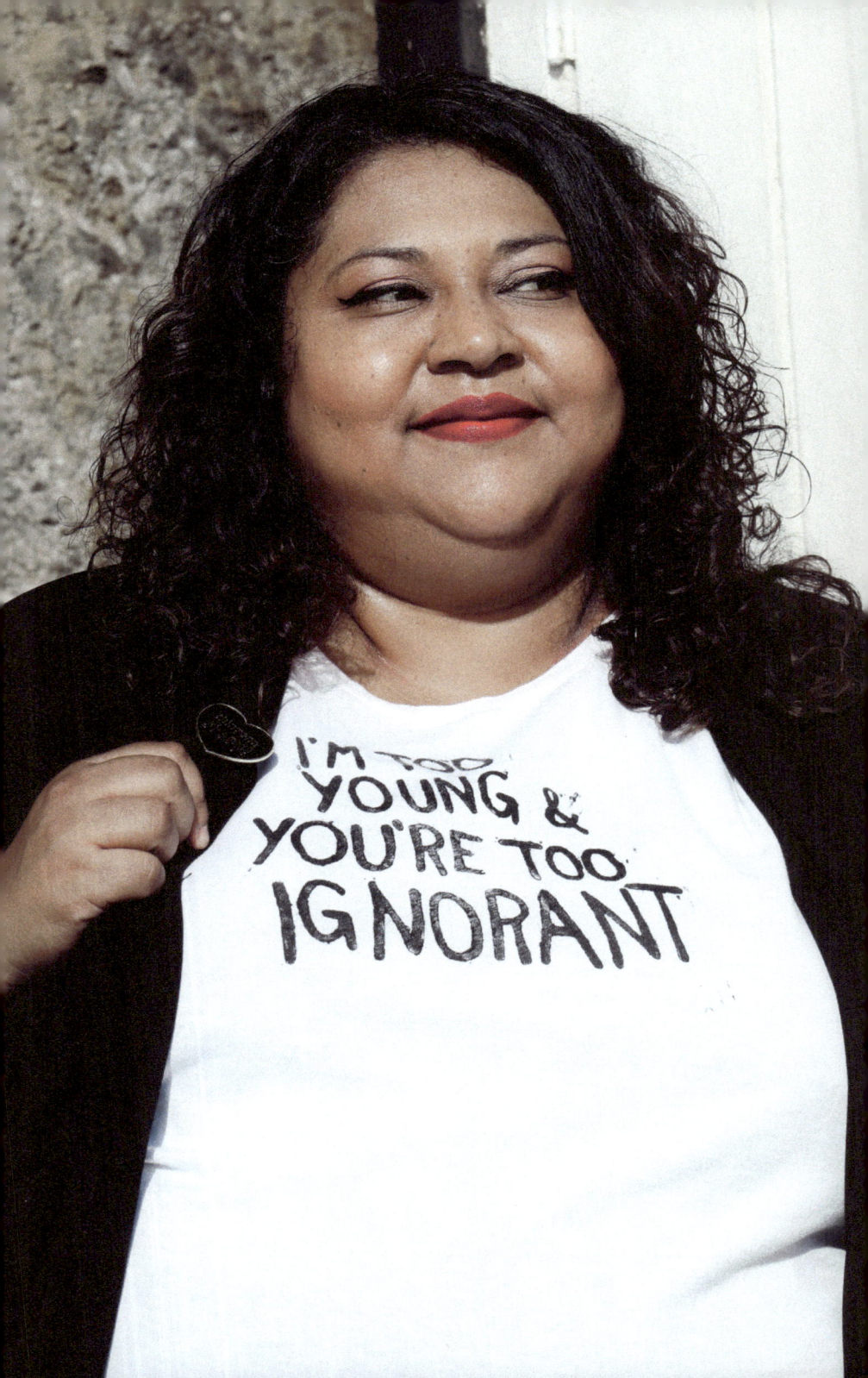

Inside Claudia Ramos' Colorful World

BRENDA HERNÁNDEZ JAIMES

From the abominable hate that has been hurled at our Latino community, we have been able to maintain our strength, and flourish to make our voices stronger. We're here, we're proud, and we're not leaving our country anytime soon. In recent years, there's been growth in having representation - it may be small, but that only fuels our motivation to continue the good fight of opening doors and making space for each other or creating new places to inspire, share, and show our beautiful culture.

"When I create, I think about what's going on in politics with Latinos getting attacked, things on the news. I feel it's my duty to create something that shows something positive and empowering to people," says Claudia Ramos. "I feel like I have to create things that will empower people to say, 'I'm here, I'm brown and I'm proud!' So I always feel that the work that I do should impact people."

Claudia Ramos is a graphic designer and entrepreneur who was born in El Salvador. She and her family moved to Los Angeles when she was just a baby, unfortunately her older brother passed away three months after arriving at their new home and Claudia quickly took on the responsibility of being the oldest sibling to her younger sisters and going to school and graduating with a B.A. in Arts from Cal State Northridge. She shares that even though she grew up in a negative neighborhood environment in LA, she was, and still is a bubbly, happy, positive person that is enjoying life.

"I grew up in an environment that was pretty tough. In LA and the ghetto, so I was always worried about getting shot. I was in a bad neighborhood and there was drug dealers, prostitutes, so I had to grow up fast. Even though there was some negativity, there was some positive too. All those things moved me to be better and seeing people grow has influenced and inspired that I got this," she says. Claudia continues to share that it was her mother that inspired her to continue on her path of accomplishing her career goals. She grew up with traditional Latino parents, her mother stayed at home, took care and cooked for her family. Then one day, her mom wanted to work and taught herself how to drive and got a job at a factory.

"I just started seeing her doing it on her own. My parents are still married, but seeing her be independent and go through that and see that if she could do it, I can do it too. She was one of my biggest impacts," Claudia shares.

Growing up in Los Angeles, Claudia never saw herself any less than her white classmates. Her bubbly personality shined through and her positivity was and still is infectious. She also shares that she never really felt she was discriminated because of her heritage or skin color.

"I never saw myself different than the white girl that was sitting next to me. I hadn't had a situation where I felt I was being discriminated or felt I was brown and not from America. Until I was 25 and I had to do my citizenship. I needed to pass this test and right there I felt like I wasn't an American. My whole time in high school and middle school I felt like an American and not Latina," she confesses. "I took the test and I passed it. Then I started working in my field and I started noticing certain things. I questioned it if it was because I'm brown that they're moving up and I wasn't - things like that. I started noticing and I started thinking differently. Now I'm a proud Latina and I started changing my designs from cute, little unicorns to 'I'm Brown and Proud', 'I'm Latina, Cabrona y Chingona'."

Her goal is to leave a legacy and to continue inspiring her community. Through her design shop, Claudia Ramos Designs, her vibrant and cute prints, pins, embroidery, and stickers, Claudia provides a small yet powerful tool to motivate and empower our community to show our love, pride, and represent each other in white spaces. Just like her keychain, Homegirl Making Moves, Claudia has seen the impact that her designs give to Latina women that work with her at Hasbro.

"At work, I have two ladies that I consider my moms. When they saw the two keychains that I did, [Homegirl Making Moves & Cabrona y Bonita] they were like, 'Oh my god! Let me see your keychain' and they saw it said, Cabrona y Bonita and they were like, 'Claudia! It says cabrona!' and they loved it," she laughs. "I explained that I know it's a bad word, but the way we're using it's like a badass woman. They each bought two keychains to gift for their daughters! That made me feel so great! Because they're kind of old school and for them to see that it's amazing and in disbelief that I did that, but they found it empowering. Little things like that make me excited to see people get empowered or feel great to be Latino or Latina. I feel like I contribute, I mean it's just me and it's a small business. For me, it's more empowering with my art."

Claudia continues to find new ways to empower her community, such as her new projects, comic illustration, Mijas Bonitas and podcast, Home Girl Chat. In Mijas Bonitas, Claudia shares she has always wanted to see representation for our women in our diverse community. In the cute world of Mijas Bonitas, one can see snaps of Claudia's childhood neighborhood where Mily, Rosa, Lizbeth, Amber, and Claudia hang out and feed their cat-us and sell paletas. She also shares about upcoming episodes of her podcast, Homegirl Chat and what she wants to provide to her listeners.

"I just want to keep it fun and real. Just represent my perspective and other females and males and bring in their own stories. A future episode will be of me sitting down with my husband and talk about his perspective of me being a breadwinner," says Claudia. "How he felt being at home, how society sees men that stay at home and see them as lazy and not doing anything. He kind of started talking about it and he even said that I even had a hard time accepting him being at home at first. He's right. Those were the arguments that we had at first. I get

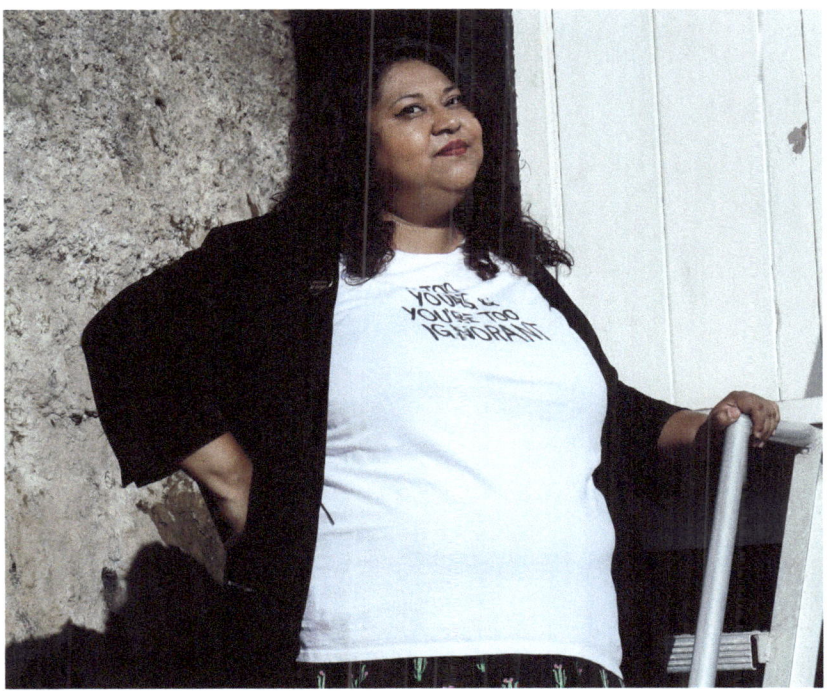

him because I had the same mentality from all the bullshit I was getting from my family," Claudia explains. "I had to accept that this is what our situation is and when I saw how he was doing an amazing job - way better than me as a father. It shed a light for me too and him. I want him to bring in his feelings and impact other men that are feeling that way or thought about it. That it's okay to be at home. Conversations that are very true and real, you don't hear a lot about."

Claudia doesn't only want to record serious conversations, she also wants to bring positive chats about people working in the creative field and how they got there. She is a creative person that loves to attend events such as conferences and summits where she meets other creative people that have inspiring stories to share. Claudia already has many people on her guest list and planning to record to release new episodes. She also shares advice to any Latinos that are interested in starting their creative path or starting their business.

"Do your research on what you want to do, but try it out. I knew I wanted to do something creative and I always loved doing illustrations and I did 'Save the Date' prints and from there I started doing pins. I did little by little and see if they worked," she advises. "Just continue from there and do your research. Ask artists how they got there, they're open to sharing how they accomplished their goals and sharing their secrets. Don't be afraid to reach out and just go for it. See from there on how it goes. We're in a good place right now even though it's very scary, we have a lot of opportunities to show and share our culture."

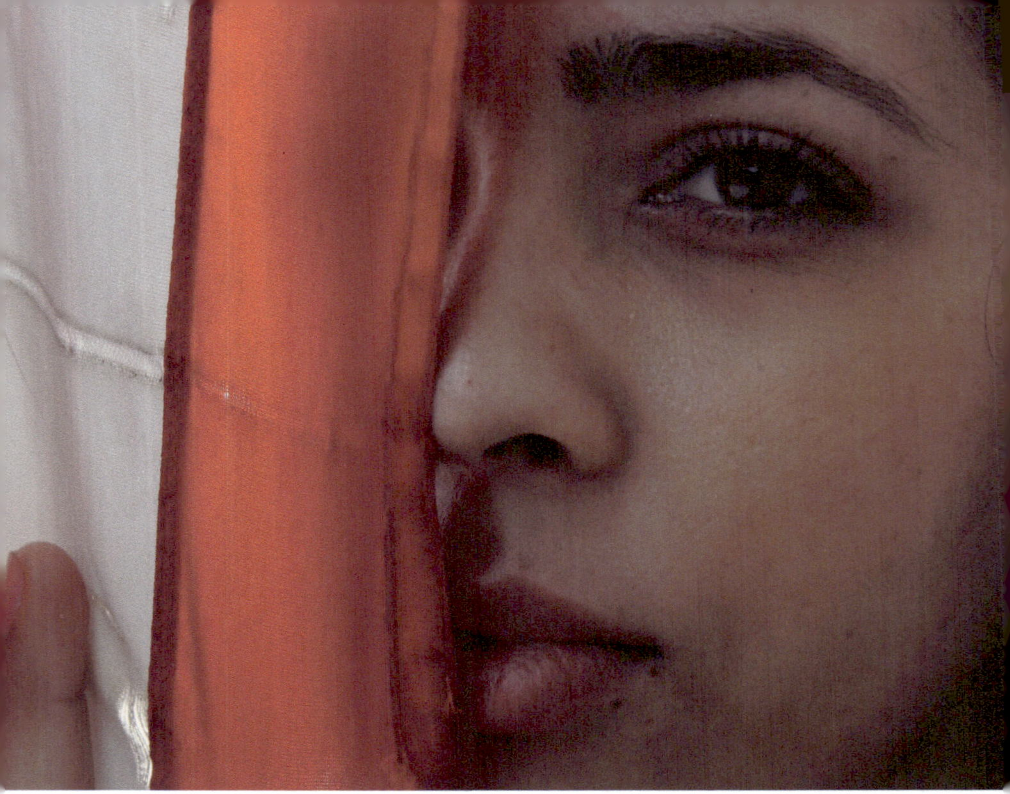

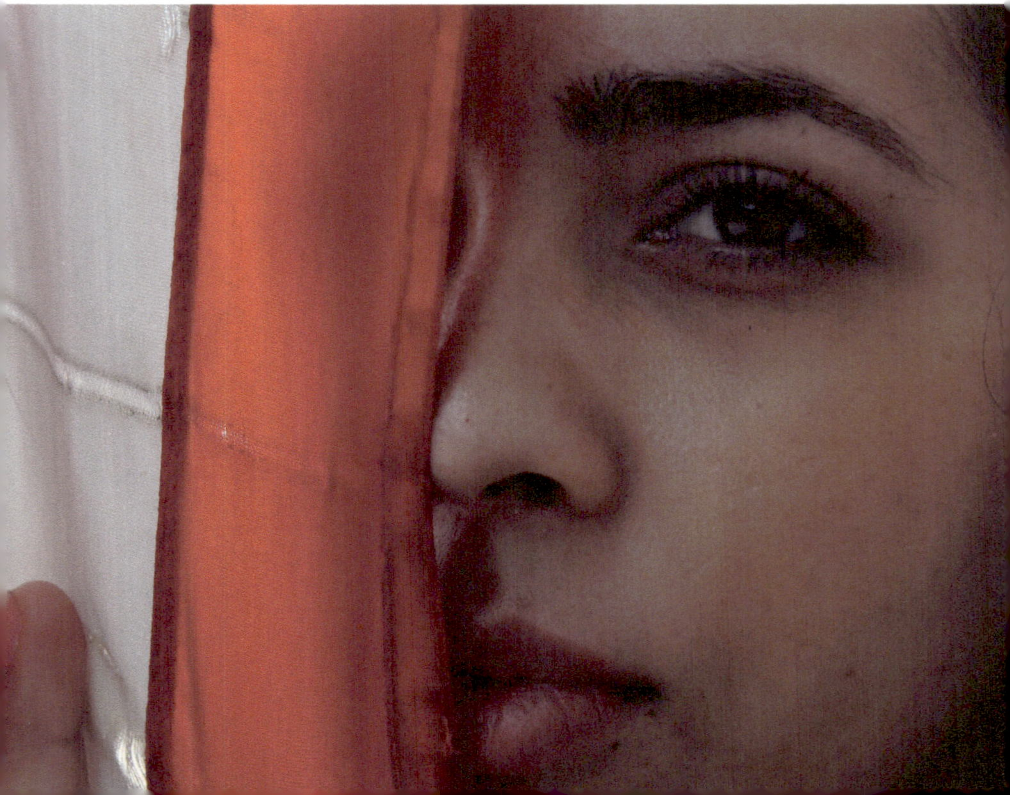

ANCHOR BABY

Eros Purizaga

they say just because you can, it doesn't mean you should.
but mom, now, how were you to know, if you ever even could?
it seems necessity's a dish best served cold when the world doesn't really care.
crossing the border where the old & new met & to this day don't agree much on
what is & isn't fair.

when we forget that borders are sometimes. & maybe even most times, what we
tend to make of them.
like an assumed cadence by a reader lost in stanza's, never fully understanding what
they truly might've meant.

although pregnant, not a doubt ran through your mind.
you never looked back from the american dream you'd gift your sons with you were
hoping to find.

assured with the faith that we're all invited to drink of God's wine, which they've
somehow confused with "God's whine",
& took control of His image; our freedom.

so now we've become the blind leading the less blind, while trying to simultaneously
outshine everyone in a reversed garden of eden.

reversed because now immigrants are accused for something of which has no real
resolution.
caught in constant tension between being fed foolish lies or needing a real
revolution.

mother your pain; your biggest blessing. that's what's odd to me.
& my shame is sometimes acting like i don't appreciate this american dream.

even in my poetry everything is purple.
i'm the outsider trying to find a peace within; like a square around a circle.

so maybe they'll never know what it feels like to be too filled with adrenaline to even
cry.
& to be told to not look up at night, because your eyes will shine.

but here i am an anchor baby with a family of faith praying for my self-proclaimed
enemy as my god tells me to.
ruining the party by telling the old news that he loves the gentile just as much as
every jew.

Photo by Josephine Jael Jimenez

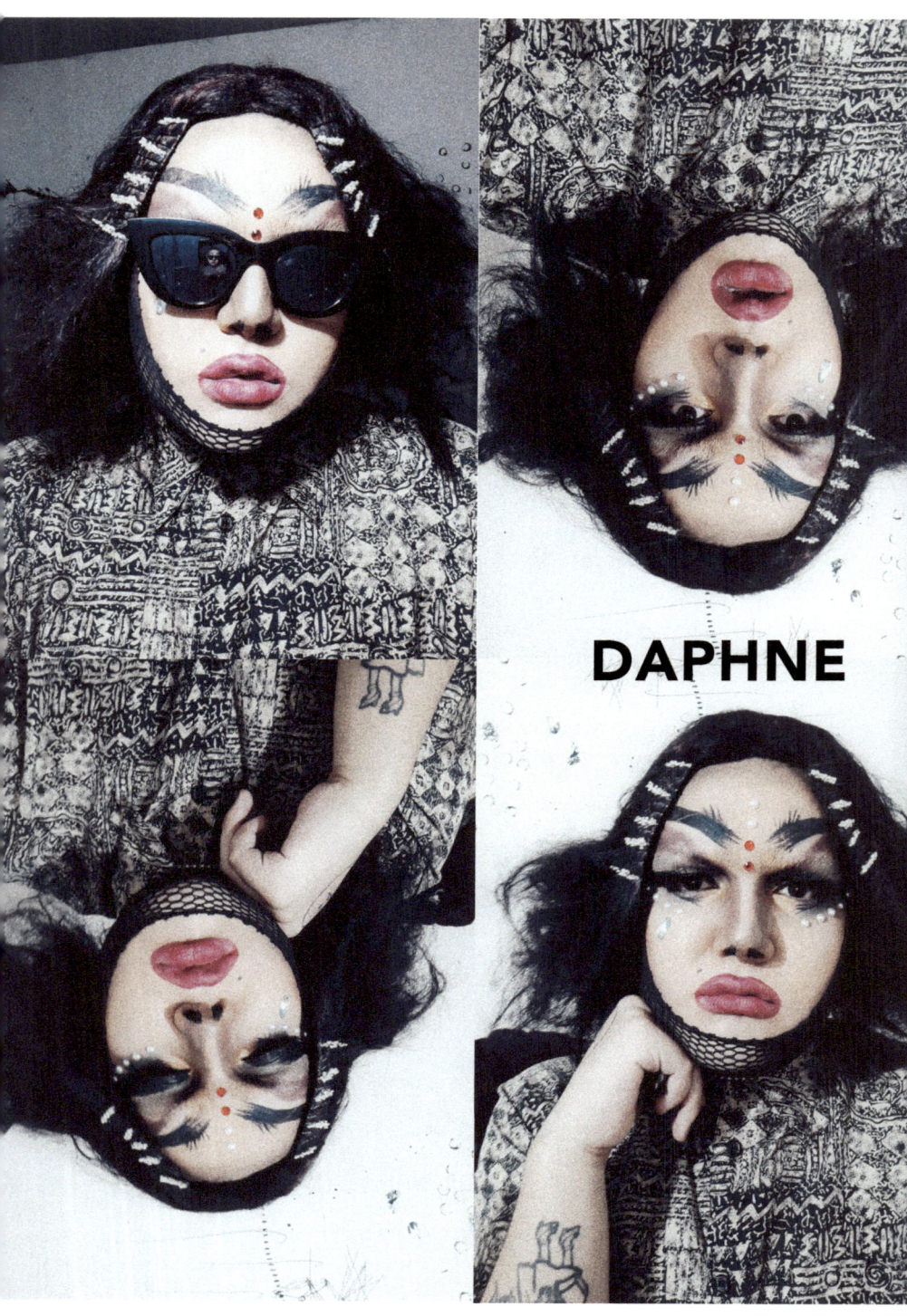

Photos by *Daphne*

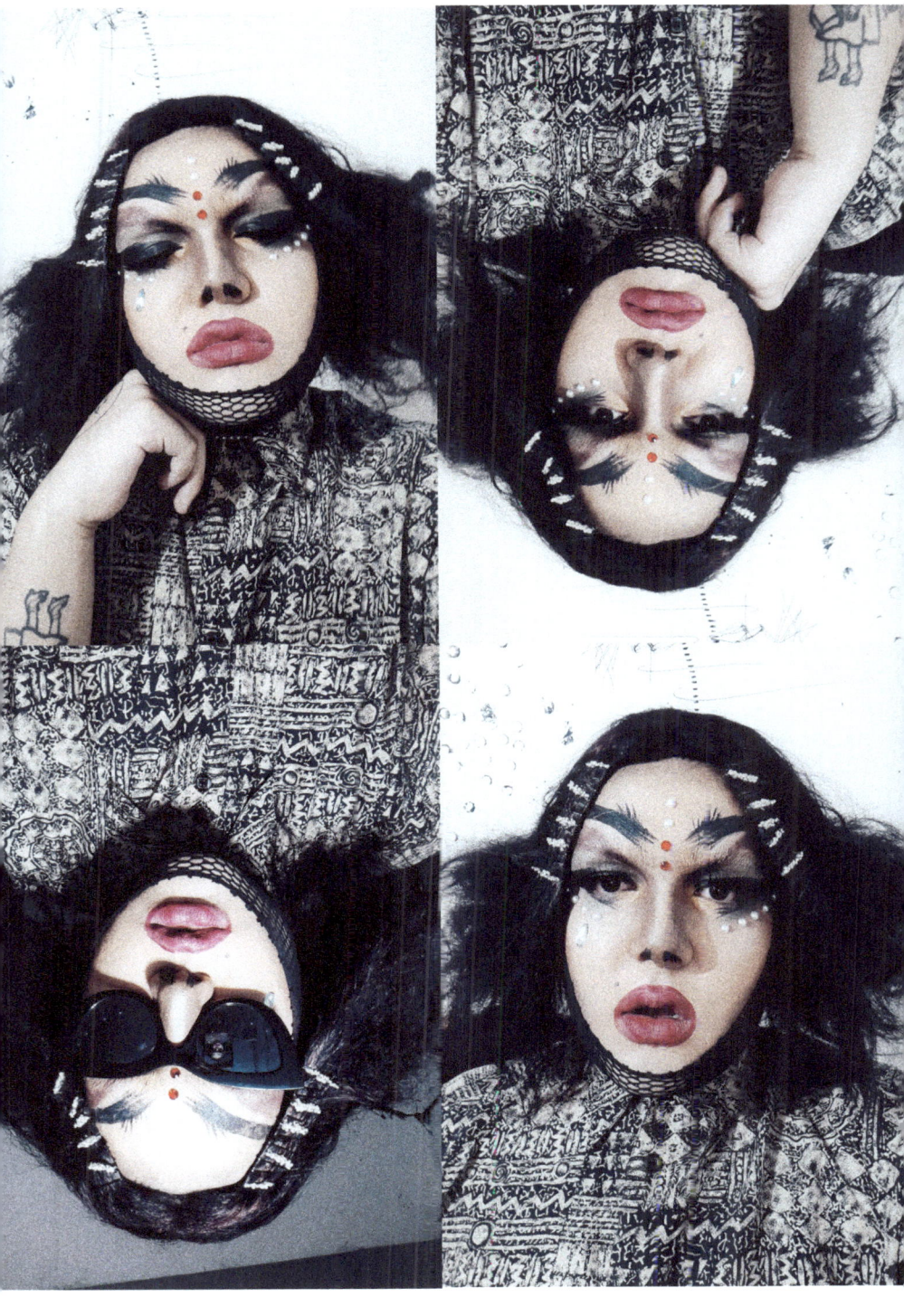

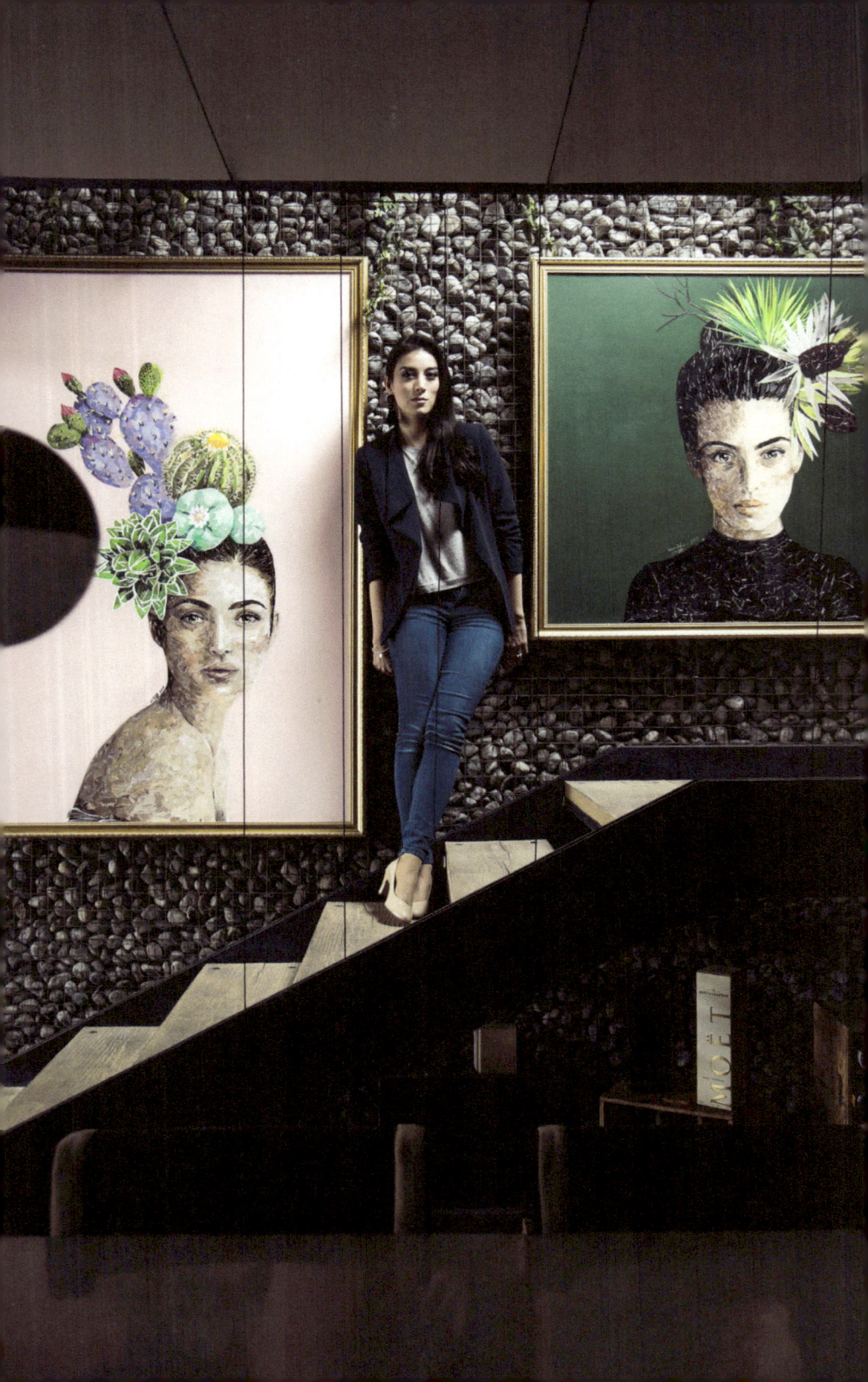

Discovering Your Sacred Paradise With Victoria Molina Vargas' Collages

BRENDA HERNÁNDEZ JAIMES

When you come across the art of Mexican artist, Victoria Molina Vargas, you feel as if you're being plucked from your spot and quickly immersed at the tiny details featured on her collages and paintings. At least, that's how I find myself swirling in her art. Questions about her creative process, themes, and materials she utilizes start bubbling in my mind. Having the honor of being invited into her fascinating artistic mind is a true delight and being able to discover her love for the environment, and how she re-uses resources to create her pieces is simply wonderful.

"I have always been very concerned about the environment. It's something that's a recurring theme. One of the last exhibits I made was called, Essence, and talked about how the sacred space and the nature that surrounds you can influence you," Victoria shares and goes into detail about her paintings. "These women were a little invaded by nature, but it was in this nature that each had a different ecosystem. It wasn't just any plant, but it was an ecosystem that was important to me at a certain point in my life, the changes that I have experienced and places that left something in me, or where I was born."

As an artist that has lived in many different cities and countries, Victoria not only paints of where she's been, but she's also acquired each lesson to her work ethic that every city has gifted her. While studying Industrial Design at the University of Monterrey, Victoria shares that living in an entrepreneurial city made her acquire a strong sense of initiating and completing her work. During her time in Torino, Italy, she acquired a taste for functional aesthetics that are extraordinary made, but it was in Kyoto, Japan, where Victoria's life completely changed.

"It was an experience that marked me for life. Before going to Japan, I had this idea of working with artisans and when I returned to Mexico, I still wanted to, but I had all these ideas that I didn't want to express them through design and I came back with the idea of continue making art," she says happily. Born in Durango, Mexico, Victoria had always been a creative person that painted from a young age, but her parents persuaded her to study Industrial Design.

"They said to me, 'Oh, don't be an artist because it's very complicated, and you're going to starve to death.' Then I studied Industrial Design

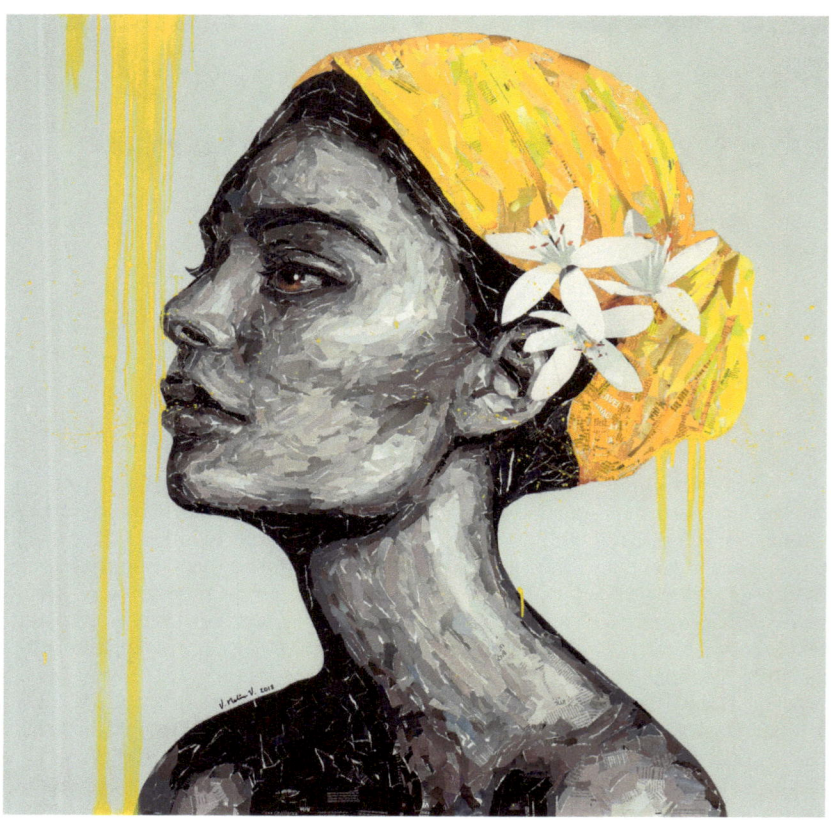

and I loved the career, it's a super amazing career, but I never left art. Art was always there. I love it and it's something I could do," Victoria states passionately. "I paint almost every day - even on Sundays. When you find something that you can do for free, then you've found your vocation. Doesn't matter how long you're in front of a canvas, I think it's cool doing what you love."

Currently living in Toluca, State of Mexico, Victoria sees the city as her sacred space and one can see the imprint that Toluca has ingrained in her collages.

"A sacred space for me is a place where you feel at home. Although I wasn't born in Toluca, for me to go to the Nevado de Toluca, is one of the most beautiful places in the world. I've been fortunate to visit many beautiful places, but I feel at home in the Nevado de Toluca. I feel that it's a magnificent, perfect place that connects you with nature which is something I myself identify with. Many of the works of the Essence series, features the snow rose that's a plant that only grows to three thousand meters above sea level and you can only find in the Nevado de Toluca," she says excitedly. "If I can identify as a plant, I would be that plant! I know the city can be cold and sometimes not very beautiful, but I'm happy to live twenty minutes from a natural paradise!"

Victoria not only describes herself as the snow rose that can withstand temperatures below zero, rocky soil, and winds that exceed 60 kilometers per hour, but she's also a creative person that is always researching in pursuit of knowledge. She loves reading about biology topics and declares that in another life, she would have been a biologist. Victoria shares that her creative process begins with her questioning about a certain plant or animal topic and quickly diving to investigating to learn. Once she has acquired the necessary information, she resurfaces with how to transmit her knowledge through her collages. Her series, Néctar, is the result of her restlessness of knowing more about the nectarivores.

"When I can't keep so many things in my head, I feel I have to expel them in a certain way. For me, it's art and what occupies most of my time. I have to get those ideas that I bring. I think that is a big part of my personality," she declares.

"In my art, I don't try to give arguments, but to question ourselves on how we react with the nature that surrounds us. Do we know or don't know her? Do we appreciate her? Do we see her or do we see her when she disappears? Or we don't realize she's gone because we never really saw her," she explains. "Néctar speaks precisely of the legacy and a comparison between the work done by bees, hummingbirds, and some mammals that eat nectar. It's in this same activity of feeding themselves that they're also generating, spreading, and transferring life. I think femininity, for me, is not so much like a pretty woman. For me, femininity represents nature a lot, it's mother nature rather than a pretty woman. This femininity that's in our surroundings and talking about these three elements of painting women, flowers, and animals are my questions about life, what surrounds us, and what we're going to leave in this world when we're gone."

Through her love for nature and art, Victoria creates her collages with unwanted magazines that are no longer of use to most people in this world, but to her it's a gift to reuse this unwanted materials to present them in a different light.

"For me, printed magazines are a waste, we're seeing less of them than before. Magazines were treasures for many people. They took care of them because it was their magazines! Right now in this digital world, we live in nobody wants magazines. And if I have a lot of magazines, they're garbage, but they're a better ecological material than oil paint. It's a destruction and construction. I destroy something to build something completely new," she smiles. "That collage process is also a time capsule where you leave things. If you approach one of my paintings you can see dates and addresses or old ads for old tech devices. For me, it's using this material to close a cycle of what matters to me and leave people with a message or a question that I want people to feel or begin to wonder when they come across my work."

Alejandra Cárcamo, @ale_versos, mercaditocorazon.com
Areli Arellano, @yosoyareli, areliarellano.com
Brenda Hernández Jaimes, Editor and Head Writer, @bren_jai
Claudia Ramos, @claudiaramosdesigns, @homegirlchat, @holamijasbonitas
Daphne, @daphnekween
Ellas, @ellasthepodcast
Eros Purizaga, @mynameiseros
Joey Reyes, @joeykangarooooo
Josephine Jael Jimenez, Editor & Designer-in-Chief, @josietakestheworld
Matt Brady, @matt.plants
Melissa Arellano, @melsartpetals
Sarah Rizvi, insta: @sarahmacriz107, twitter: @sarahmacriz
Victoria Molina Vargas, @artvictoriam, victoriamolina.mx
Young Ignorantes, @youngignorantes, www.youngignorantes.com

www.ingramcontent.com/pod-product-compliance
Lightning Source LLC
Chambersburg PA
CBHW040342220526
45473CB00009B/2765